P9-BIX-654

ANIMAL RAIN

Story by
Lance Nevis

To order books please visit
www.createspace.com/3394703
or
www.animalrain.com

Illustrated by Tom Piper

© COPYRIGHT
NEVIS

This book is dedicated to my nephew Michael Robert Nevis Jr. (Mikey) who lives with Autism everyday. I would like to raise awareness and understanding about this devastating and life changing disorder. As of 2009, 1 in every 150 children will be diagnosed with Autism. Part of the proceeds from the sale of this book will go toward helping to find a cure for Mikey and many children like him.

Lance Nevis

What do you know about animal rain?

I'm sure that you've heard it before.

When clouds start to gather up over your head,

it's looking to possibly pour.

Now it's coming down "cats and dogs"

is a phrase that my dad and I used to share.

But I know that there is more to it than that,

so everyone better beware.

It starts as a trickle before it gets soggy,

A drizzle of minnows, a shower of froggys.

The gradual soaking of foxes

and voles...

...works into a downpour

of chickens and moles.

And bats and bears and crows that "caw",

will have you staring up in awe.

With every kind of beast and bird,
It's hard to put it into words.

So watch yourself or you'll get mashed,
by rhinos and hippos coming down with a crash.

You best find a grotto where you could go stay,
or hide in a cave that's out of the way.

"Cause under a shelter there's safety for you
but out in the open's an obvious zoo.

Well that is my story, I know it sounds strange.
Now go tell your friends about...animal rain.

Color your own pictures !

ANIMAL RAIN COLORING BOOK

A perfect landing in the rain.

" We'll be safe and dry in the cave."

"Look at those dark clouds."

" I remember what my dad said. "

"Hey, my nose is wet!"

What a big frog!

"Watch me slide!"

A good place to watch the rain.

" This is fun! "

" It's a zoo out there. "

" So this is animal rain! "

3849096

Made in the USA